Impressum
Verlag: BABADADA GmbH, Nedderfeld 112 , 22529 Hamburg
Geschäftsführer / Verlagsleitung: Harald Hof
Druck: Books on Demand GmbH, In de Tarpen 42, 22848 Norderstedt

Imprint
Publisher: BABADADA GmbH, Nedderfeld 112 , 22529 Hamburg, Germany
Managing Director / Publishing direction: Harald Hof
Print: Books on Demand GmbH, In de Tarpen 42, 22848 Norderstedt

school

ysgol

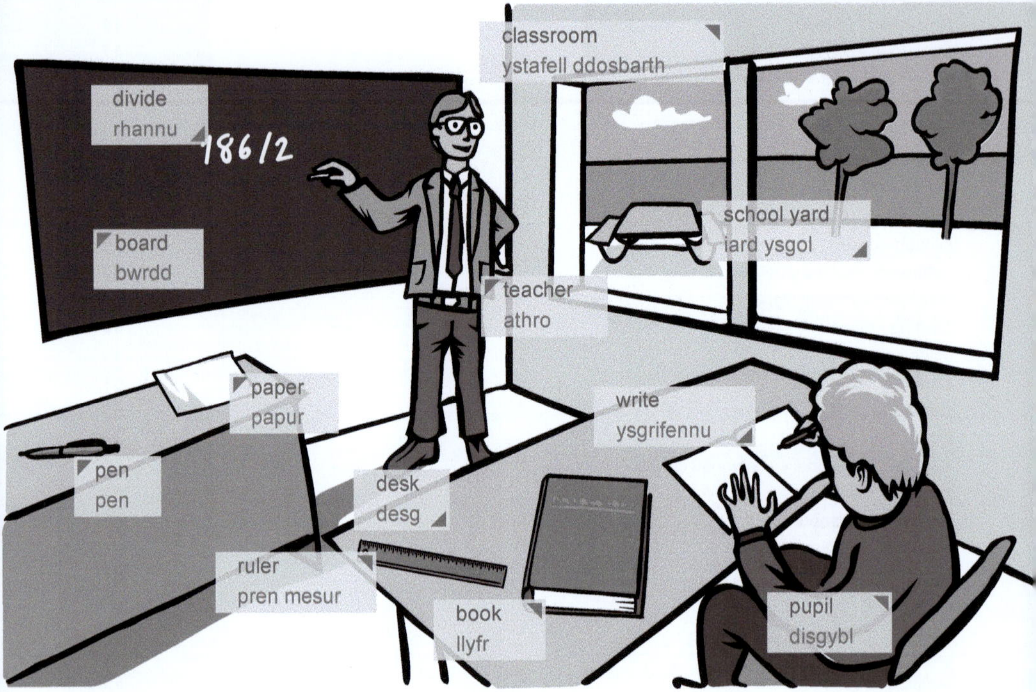
classroom
ystafell ddosbarth
divide
rhannu
186/2
board
bwrdd
school yard
iard ysgol
teacher
athro
paper
papur
write
ysgrifennu
pen
pen
desk
desg
ruler
pren mesur
book
llyfr
pupil
disgybl

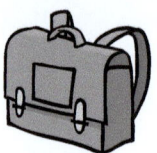

satchel

bag ysgol

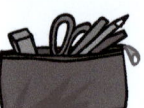

pencil case

blwch penseli

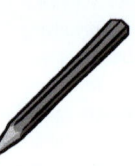

pencil

pensil

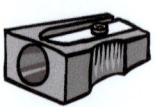

pencil sharpener

peth rhoi min ar bensil

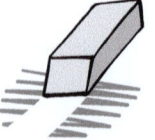

rubber

rwber

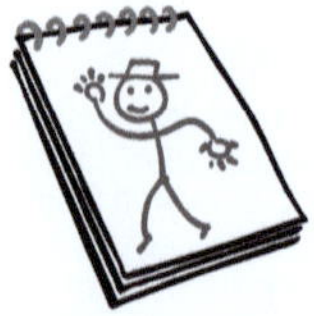

drawing pad

pad arlunio

drawing

llun

paintbrush

brws paent

paint box

blwch paent

scissors

siswrn

glue

glud

exercise book

llyfr ysgrifennu

homework

gwaith cartref

number

rhif

2+2

add

ychwanegu

5-2

subtract

tynnu

2×2

multiply

lluosi

calculate

cyfrifo

letter

llythyren

alphabet

gwyddor

word

gair

text

testun

read

darllen

chalk

sialc

lesson

gwers

register

cofrestr

examination

arholiad

certificate

tystysgrif

school uniform

gwisg ysgol

education

addysg

encyclopedia

gwyddoniadur

university

prifysgol

microscope

microsgop

map

map

waste-paper basket

basged papur gwastraff

hotel
gwesty

hostel
hostel

ROOMS

currency exchange office
swyddfa gyfnewid

EXCHANGE

car
car

language

iaith

yes / no

ie / na

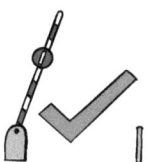

Okay

iawn

hello

helo

translator

cyfieithydd

Thank you

Diolch yn fawr

how much is...?

faint yw ...?

I don't get it

Dw i ddim yn deall

problem

problem

Good evening!

Noswaith dda!

Good morning!

Bore da!

Good night!

Nos da!

goodbye

hwyl

direction

cyfarwyddyd

luggage

bagiau

bag

bag

backpack

gwarbac

guest

gwestai

room

ystafell

sleeping bag

sach gysgu

tent

pabell

tourist information

gwybodaeth i ymwelwyr

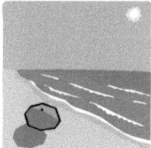

beach

traeth

credit card

cerdyn credyd

breakfast

brecwast

lunch

cinio

dinner

swper

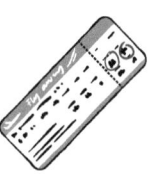

Ticket

tocyn

elevator

lifft

stamp

stamp

border

ffin

customs

tollau

embassy

llysgenhadaeth

visa

fisa

passport

pasbort

travel - teithio

transport
cludiant

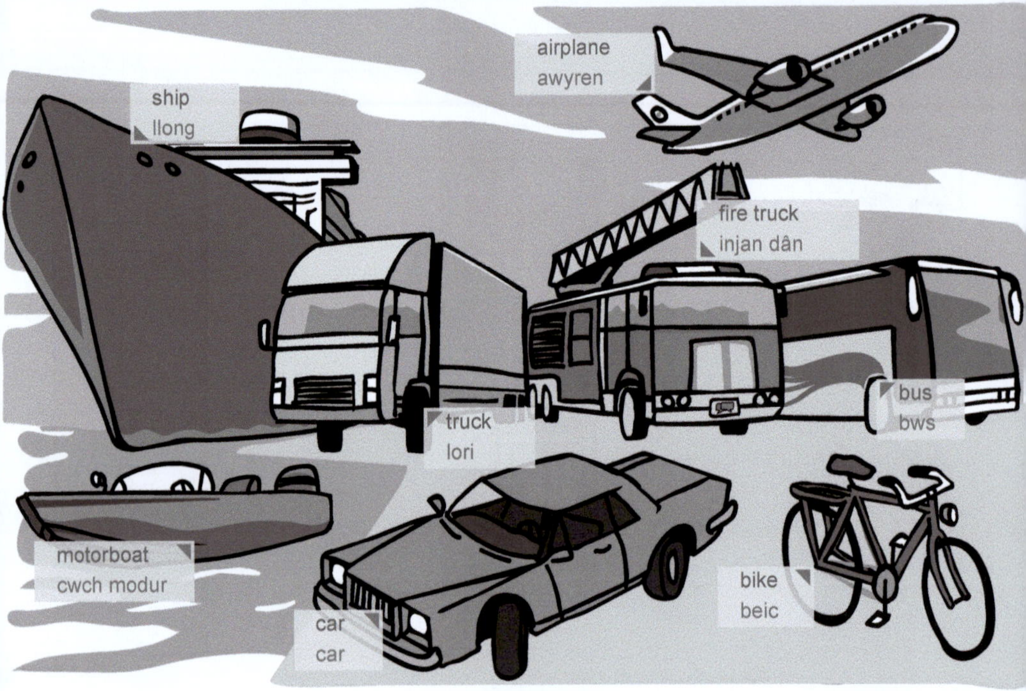
airplane
awyren
ship
llong
fire truck
injan dân
bus
bws
truck
lori
motorboat
cwch modur
car
car
bike
beic

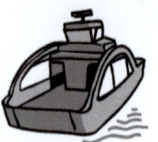

ferry

fferi

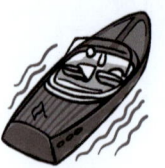

boat

cwch

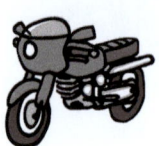

motorbike

beic modur

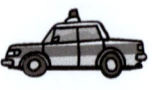

police car

car yr heddlu

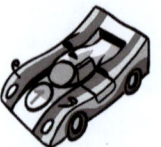

racing car

car rasio

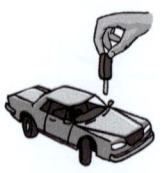

rental car

car wedi'i rentu

car sharing

rhannu car

tow truck

lori tynnu

garbage truck

lori ysbwriel

engine

modur

fuel

tanwydd

fuel station

gorsaf betrol

traffic sign

arwydd traffig

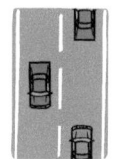

traffic

traffig

traffic jam

tagfa draffig

parking lot

maes parcio

train station

gorsaf drennau

tracks

traciau

train

trên

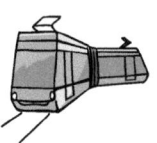

tram

tram

wagon

wagen

helicopter

hofrennydd

airport

maes awyr

tower

tŵr

passenger

teithiwr

container

cynhwysydd

carton

paced

cart

cert

basket

basged

take off / land

esgyn / glanio

city

dinas

village

pentref

city center

canol y ddinas

house

tŷ

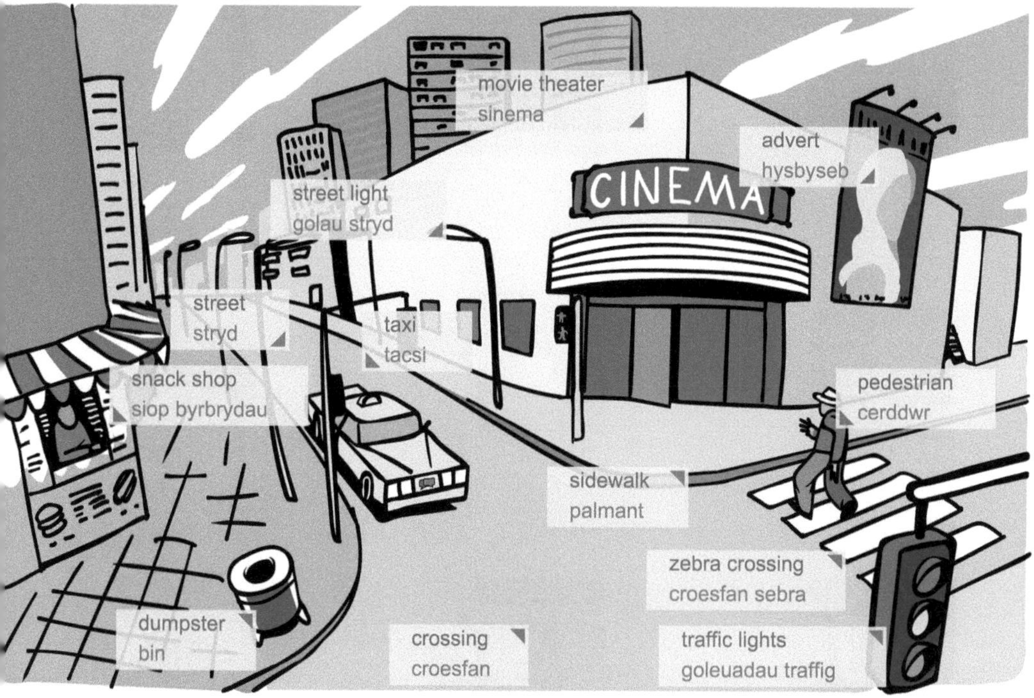

movie theater
sinema

advert
hysbyseb

street light
golau stryd

CINEMA

street
stryd

taxi
tacsi

snack shop
siop byrbrydau

pedestrian
cerddwr

sidewalk
palmant

zebra crossing
croesfan sebra

dumpster
bin

crossing
croesfan

traffic lights
goleuadau traffig

hut

cwt

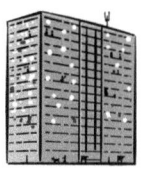

apartment

fflat

train station

gorsaf drennau

city hall

neuadd y dref

museum

amgueddfa

school

ysgol

university

prifysgol

bank

banc

hospital

ysbyty

hotel

gwesty

pharmacy

fferyllfa

office

swyddfa

book shop

siop lyfrau

shop

siop

flower shop

siop flodau

supermarket

archfarchnad

market

farchnad

department store

siop adrannol

fishmonger's shop

siop bysgod

mall

canolfan siopa

harbor

harbwr

park

parc

bench

banc

bridge

pont

stairs

grisiau

subway

rheilffordd danddaearol

tunnel

twnnel

bus stop

safle bws

bar

bar

restaurant

bwyty

postbox

blwch post

street sign

arwydd stryd

parking meter

mesurydd parcio

zoo

sŵ

swimming pool

pwll nofio

mosque

mosg

city - dinas

farm

fferm

pollution

llygredd

cemetery

mynwent

church

eglwys

playground

maes chwarae

temple

teml

landscape

tirwedd

signpost
arwydd cyfeirio

path
ffordd

meadow
dôl

stone
carreg

tree
coeden

hiker
heiciwr

river
afon

grass
glaswellt

flower
blodyn

valley

cwm

hill

bryn

lake

llyn

forest

coedwig

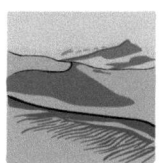

desert

anialwch

volcano

llosgfynydd

castle

castell

rainbow

enfys

mushroom

madarchen

palm tree

palmwydden

mosquito

mosgito

fly

pryf

ant

morgrugyn

bee

gwenyn

spider

pryf copyn

beetle

chwilen

frog

llyffant

squirrel

gwiwer

hedgehog

draenog

hare

ysgyfarnog

owl

tylluan

bird

aderyn

swan

alarch

boar

baedd

deer

carw

moose

elc

dam

argae

wind turbine

tyrbin gwynt

solar panel

panel haul

climate

hinsawdd

restaurant
bwyty

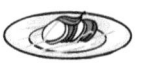

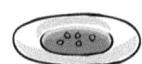

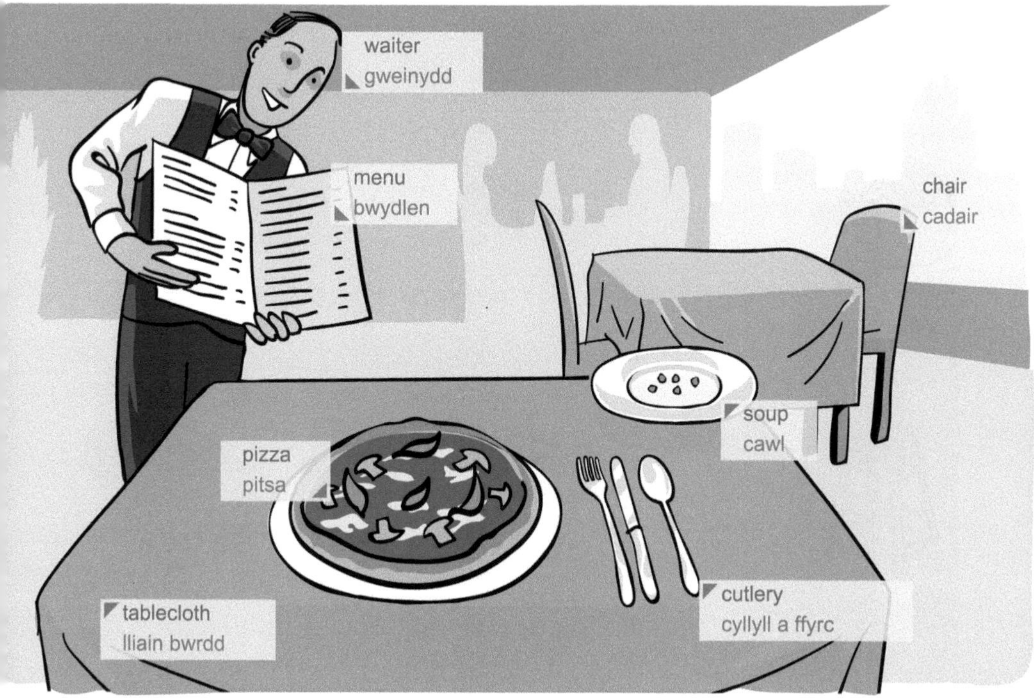
waiter
gweinydd
menu
bwydlen
chair
cadair
soup
cawl
pizza
pitsa
tablecloth
lliain bwrdd
cutlery
cyllyll a ffyrc

starter

cwrs cyntaf

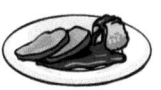

main course

prif gwrs

dessert

pwdin

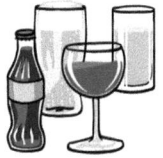

drinks

diodydd

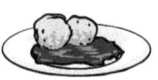

food

bwyd

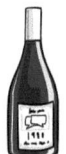

bottle

potel

fast food

bwyd cyflym

street food

bwyd y stryd

teapot

tebot

sugar bowl

powlen siwgr

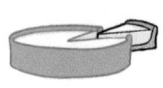

portion

dogn

espresso machine

peiriant espresso

high chair

cadair plentyn

bill

bil

tray

hambwrdd

knife

cyllell

fork

fforc

spoon

llwy

teaspoon

llwy de

serviette

napcyn

glass

gwydr

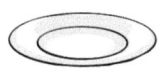

plate

plât

soup plate

plât cawl

saucer

soser

sauce

saws

salt shaker

pot halen

pepper mill

melin bupur

vinegar

finegr

oil

olew

spices

sbeisys

ketchup

saws coch

mustard

mwstard

mayonnaise

mayonnaise

supermarket
archfarchnad

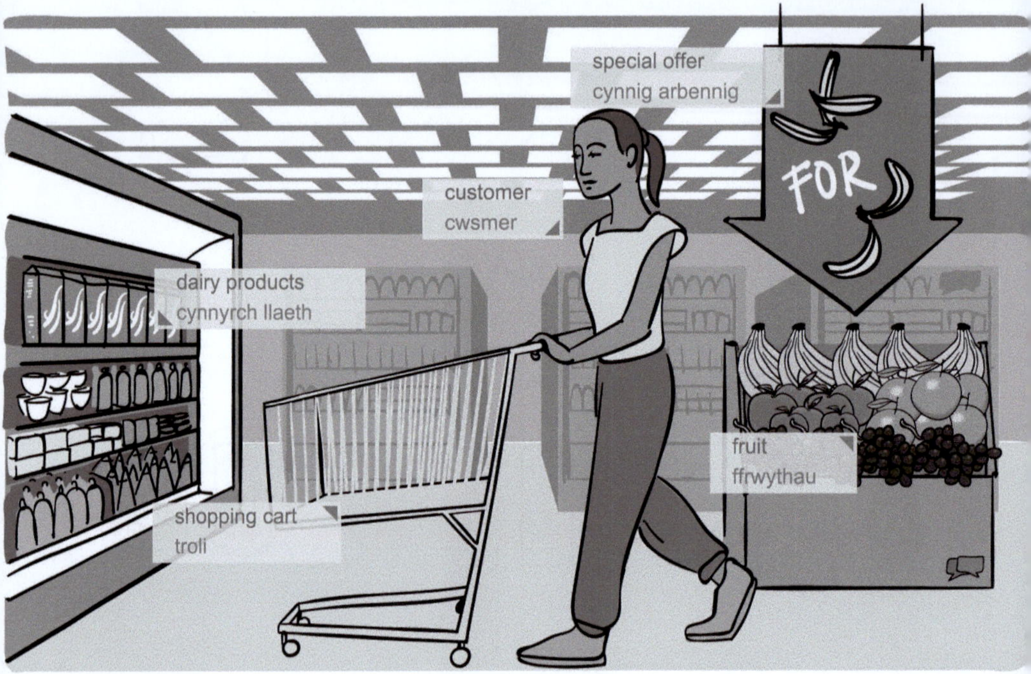
special offer
cynnig arbennig
FOR
customer
cwsmer
dairy products
cynnyrch llaeth
fruit
ffrwythau
shopping cart
troli

BUTCHERS

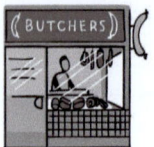

butcher's shop

siop gig

BAKERY

bakery

siop fara

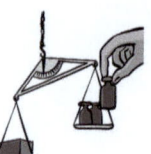

weigh

pwyso

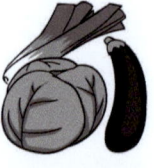

vegetables

llysiau

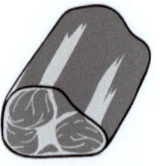

meat

cig

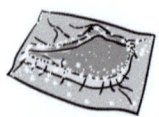

frozen food

Bwyd wedi'i rewi

cold cuts

cig oer

canned food

bwyd tun

detergent

powdr golchi

candy

da-da

household products

cynnyrch cartref

cleaning products

cynhyrchion glanhau

sales representative

gwerthwraig

cash register

til

cashier

ariannwr

shopping list

rhestr siopa

opening hours

oriau agor

wallet

waled

credit card

cerdyn credyd

bag

bag

plastic bag

bag plastig

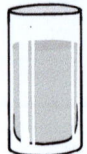

water
dŵr

juice
sudd

milk
llefrith

coke
côc

wine
gwin

beer
cwrw

alcohol
alcohol

cocoa
coco

tea
te

coffee
coffi

espresso
espresso

cappuccino
cappuccino

banana

ffrwchledd

apple

afal

orange

oren

melon

melon

lemon

lemwn

carrot

moronen

garlic

garlleg

bamboo

bambŵ

onion

nionyn

mushroom

madarchen

nuts

cnau

noodles

nwdls

spaghetti

sbageti

rice

reis

salad

salad

fries

sglodion

fried potatoes

tatws wedi'u ffrïo

pizza

pitsa

hamburger

hambyrger

sandwich

brechdan

escalope

cytled

ham

ham

salami

salami

sausage

selsig

chicken

cyw iâr

roast

rhost

fish

pysgodyn

porridge oats

ceirch uwd

muesli

miwsli

cornflakes

creision ŷd

flour

blawd

croissant

croissant

bread roll

bynsen

bread

bara

toast

tost

cookies

bisgedi

butter

menyn

curd

ceuled

cake

teisen

egg

wy

fried egg

wy wedi'i ffrïo

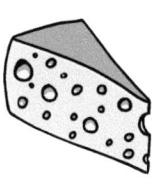

cheese

caws

ice cream

hufen iâ

sugar

siwgr

honey

mêl

jelly

jam

nougat cream

siocled taenu

curry

cyri

farm
fferm

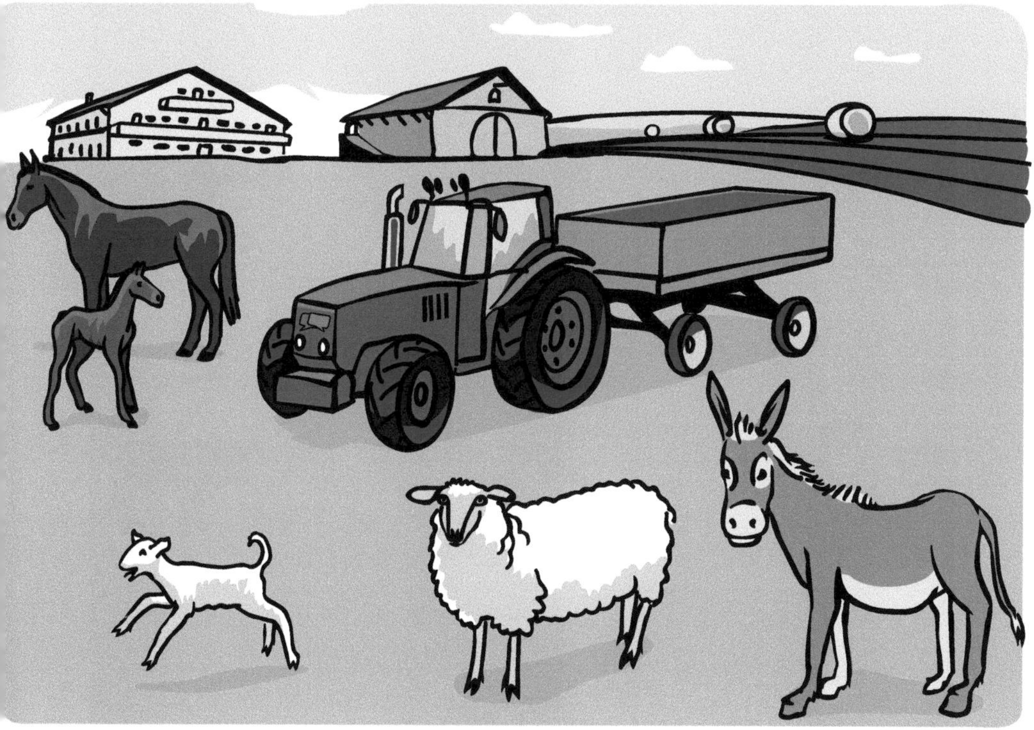

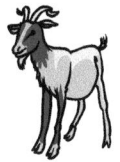

goat
gafr

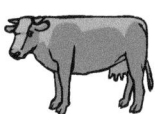

cow
buwch

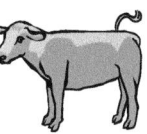

calf
llo

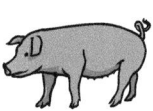

pig
mochyn

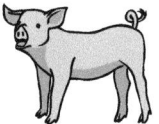

piglet
porchell

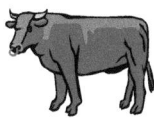

bull
tarw

goose

gwydd

duck

hwyaden

chick

cyw

hen

iâr

cockerel

ceiliog

rat

llygoden fawr

cat

cath

mouse

llygoden

ox

ych

dog

ci

dog house

cwt ci

garden hose

pibell ddŵr

watering can

can dŵr

scythe

pladur

plow

aradr

sickle

cryman

hoe

fforch chwynu

pitchfork

picwarch

axe

bwyell

pushcart

berfa

trough

cafn

milk can

tun llefrith

sack

sach

fence

ffens

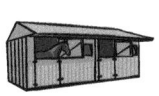
stable

stabl

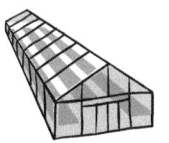
greenhouse

tŷ gwydr

soil

pridd

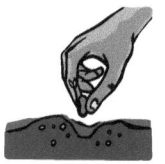
seed

hedyn

fertilizer

gwrtaith

combine harvester

dyrnwr medi

harvest

cynaeafu

harvest

cynhaeaf

yams

iamau

wheat

gwenith

soya

soi

potato

tysen

corn

grawn

rapeseed

had rêp

fruit tree

coeden ffrwythau

manioc

manioc

grain

grawnfwydydd

house

tŷ

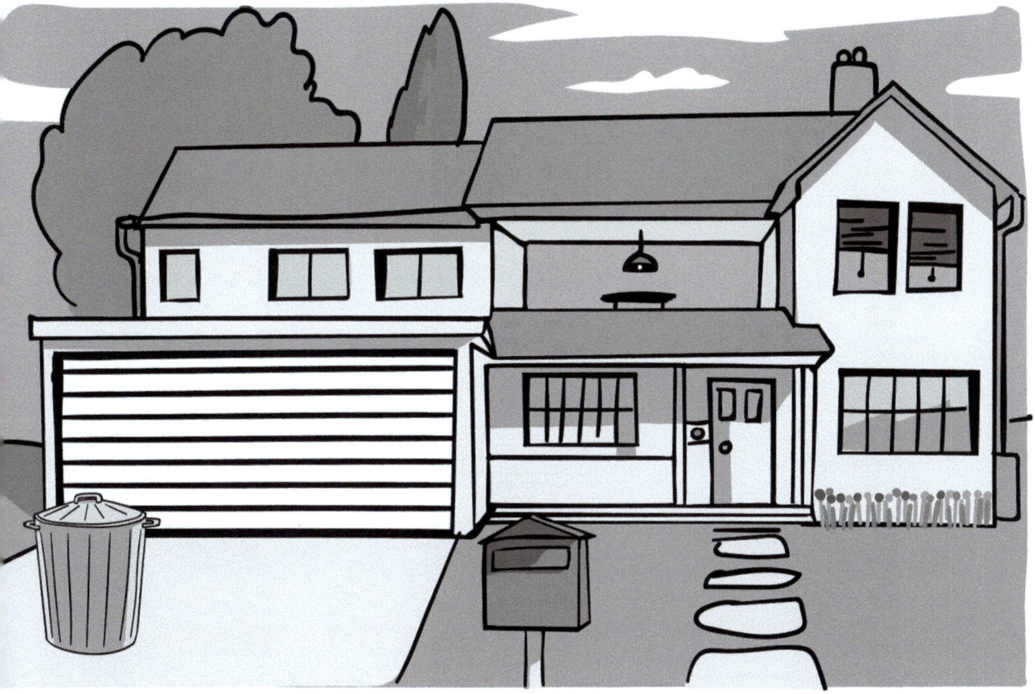

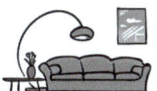

living room

lolfa

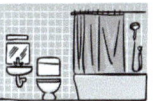

bathroom

ystafell ymolchi

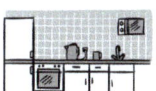

kitchen

cegin

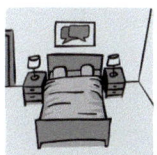

bedroom

ystafell wely

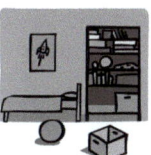

kids room

ystafell plentyn

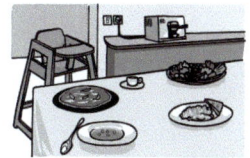

dining room

ystafell fwyta

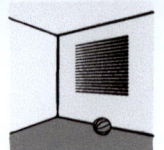

floor

llawr

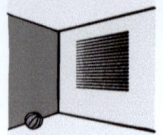

wall

wal

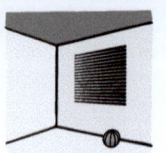

ceiling

nenfwd

cellar

seler

sauna

sawna

balcony

balconi

terrace

teras

pool

pwll

lawn mower

peiriant torri gwair

sheet

taflen

bedspread

gorchudd gwely

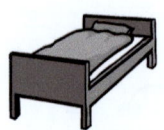

bed

gwely

broom

ysgub

bucket

bwced

switch

swits

carpet

carped

drape

llen

table

bwrdd

chair

cadair

rocking chair

cadair siglo

armchair

cadair freichiau

book

llyfr

blanket

blanced

decoration

addurn

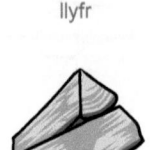

firewood

coed tân

film

ffilm

stereo system

hi-fi

key

agoriad

newspaper

papur newydd

painting

darlun

poster

poster

radio

radio

notebook

llyfr nodiadau

vacuum cleaner

hwfer

cactus

cactws

candle

cannwyll

kitchen
cegin

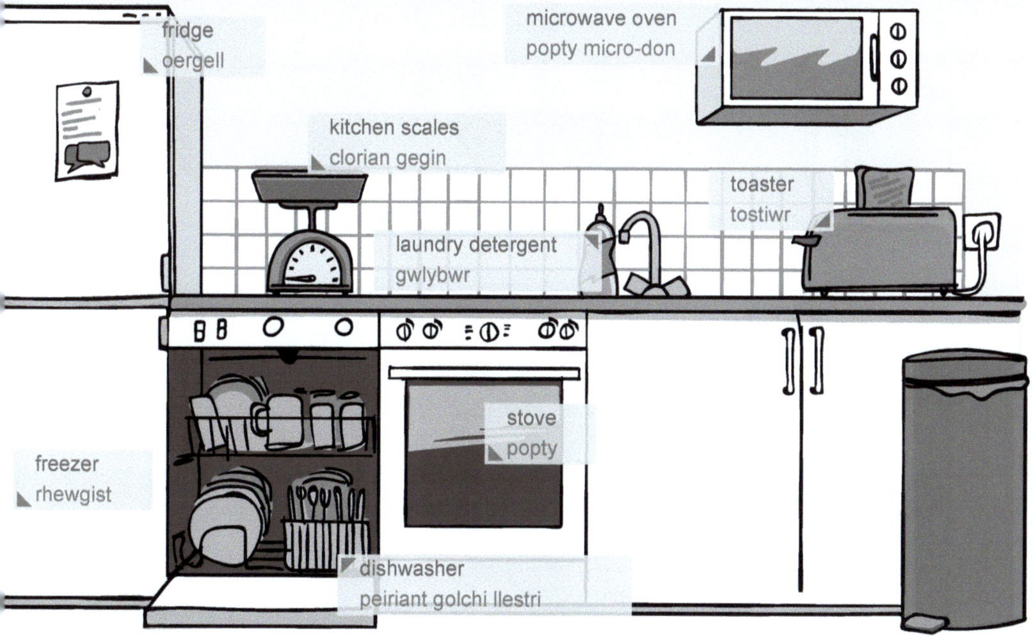
fridge
oergell
microwave oven
popty micro-don
kitchen scales
clorian gegin
toaster
tostiwr
laundry detergent
gwlybwr
stove
popty
freezer
rhewgist
dishwasher
peiriant golchi llestri

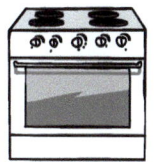

cooker
popty

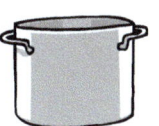

pot
pot

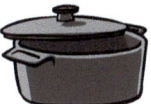

cast-iron pot
pot haearn bwrw

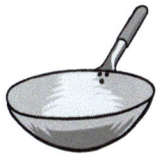

wok / kadai
wok / kadai

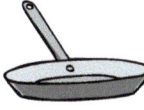

pan
padell

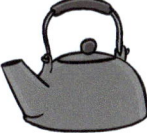

kettle
tegell

steamer

sosban stemio

baking tray

hambwrdd pobi

crockery

llestri

mug

mwg

bowl

powlen

chopsticks

gweill bwyta

ladle

lletwad

spatula

ysbodol

whisk

chwisg

strainer

hidlydd

sieve

gogr

grater

gratiwr

mortar

morter

barbecue

barbeciw

fireplace

tân agored

chopping board

bwrdd torri cig

rolling pin

rholbren

corkscrew

tynnwr corcyn

can

tun

can opener

peth agor tuniau

oven cloth

clwt pot

sink

sinc

brush

brws

sponge

sbwng

blender

peiriant cymysgu

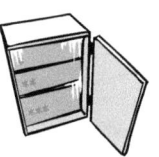

deep freezer

rhewgell

baby bottle

potel babi

tap

tap

bathroom

ystafell ymolchi

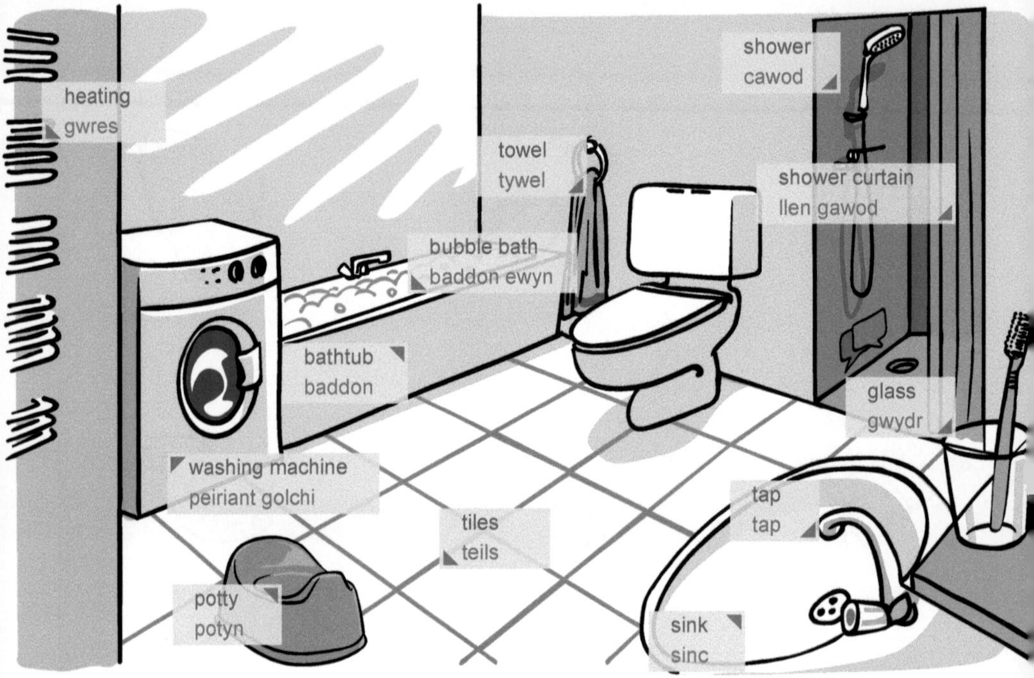

shower
cawod
heating
gwres
towel
tywel
shower curtain
llen gawod
bubble bath
baddon ewyn
bathtub
baddon
glass
gwydr
washing machine
peiriant golchi
tap
tap
tiles
teils
potty
potyn
sink
sinc

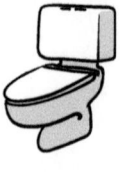

toilet

tŷ bach

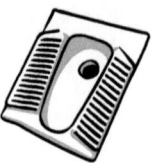

squat toilet

toiled cyrcydu

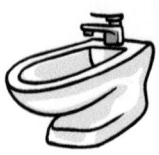

bidet

bidet

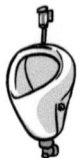

urinal

troethfa

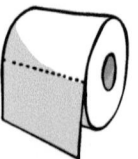

toilet paper

papur tŷ bach

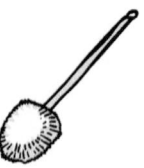

toilet brush

brws tŷ bach

toothbrush

brws dannedd

toothpaste

past dannedd

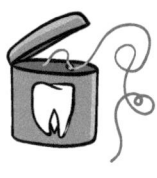

dental floss

edau ddannedd

wash

golchi

hand shower

cawod llaw

douche

golchfa

basin

basn

back brush

brws-ôl

soap

sebon

shower gel

gel cawod

shampoo

siampŵ

flannel

gwlanen

drain

ffos

creme

hufen

deodorant

diaroglydd

mirror

drych

hand mirror

drych llaw

razor

rasel

shaving foam

ewyn eillio

aftershave

sent eillio

comb

crib

brush

brws

hair-dryer

sychwr gwallt

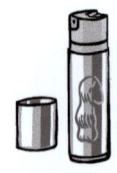

hairspray

chwistrell gwallt

makeup

colur

lipstick

minlliw

nail varnish

farnais ewinedd

cotton wool

gwlân cotwm

nail scissors

siswrn ewinedd

perfume

persawr

washbag

bag ymolchi

stool

stôl

weighing scales

clorian

bathrobe

gŵn baddon

rubber gloves

menig rwber

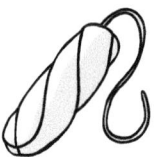

tampon

tampon

sanitary towel

tywel misglwyf

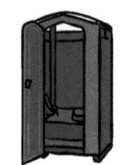

chemical toilet

toiled cemegol

kids room
ystafell plentyn

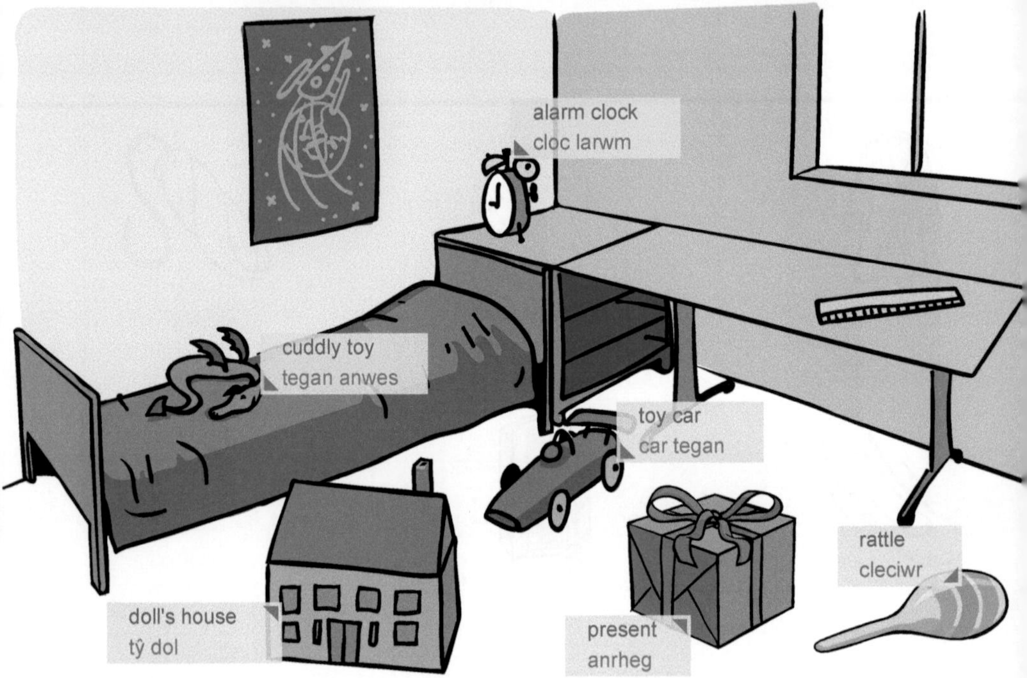
alarm clock
cloc larwm
cuddly toy
tegan anwes
toy car
car tegan
rattle
cleciwr
doll's house
tŷ dol
present
anrheg

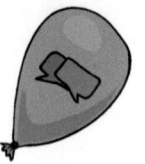

balloon

balŵn

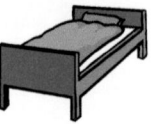

bed

gwely

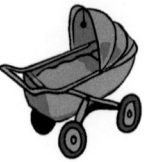

stroller

pram

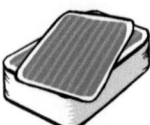

deck of cards

pecyn o gardiau

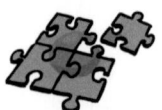

jigsaw

jig-so

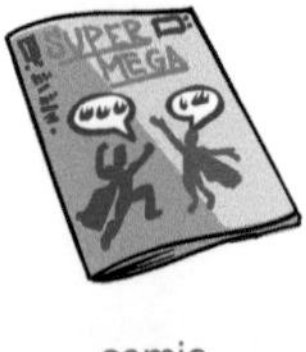

comic

comic

lego bricks

brics Lego

toy blocks

blociau adeiladu

action figure

ffigur gweithredu

romper suit

babygro

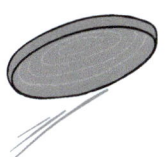

frisbee

ffrisbi

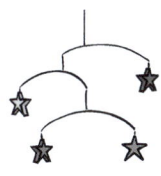

mobile

ffôn symudol

board game

gêm fwrdd

dice

deis

model train set

set model trên

pacifier

teth lwgu

party

parti

picture book

llyfr lluniau

ball

pêl

doll

dol

play

chwarae

sandpit

pwll tywod

swing

swing

toys

teganau

video game console

consol gemau fideo

tricycle

beic tair olwyn

teddy bear

tedi

wardrobe

cwpwrdd dillad

clothing

dillad

socks

hosanau

stockings

hosanau

tights

teits

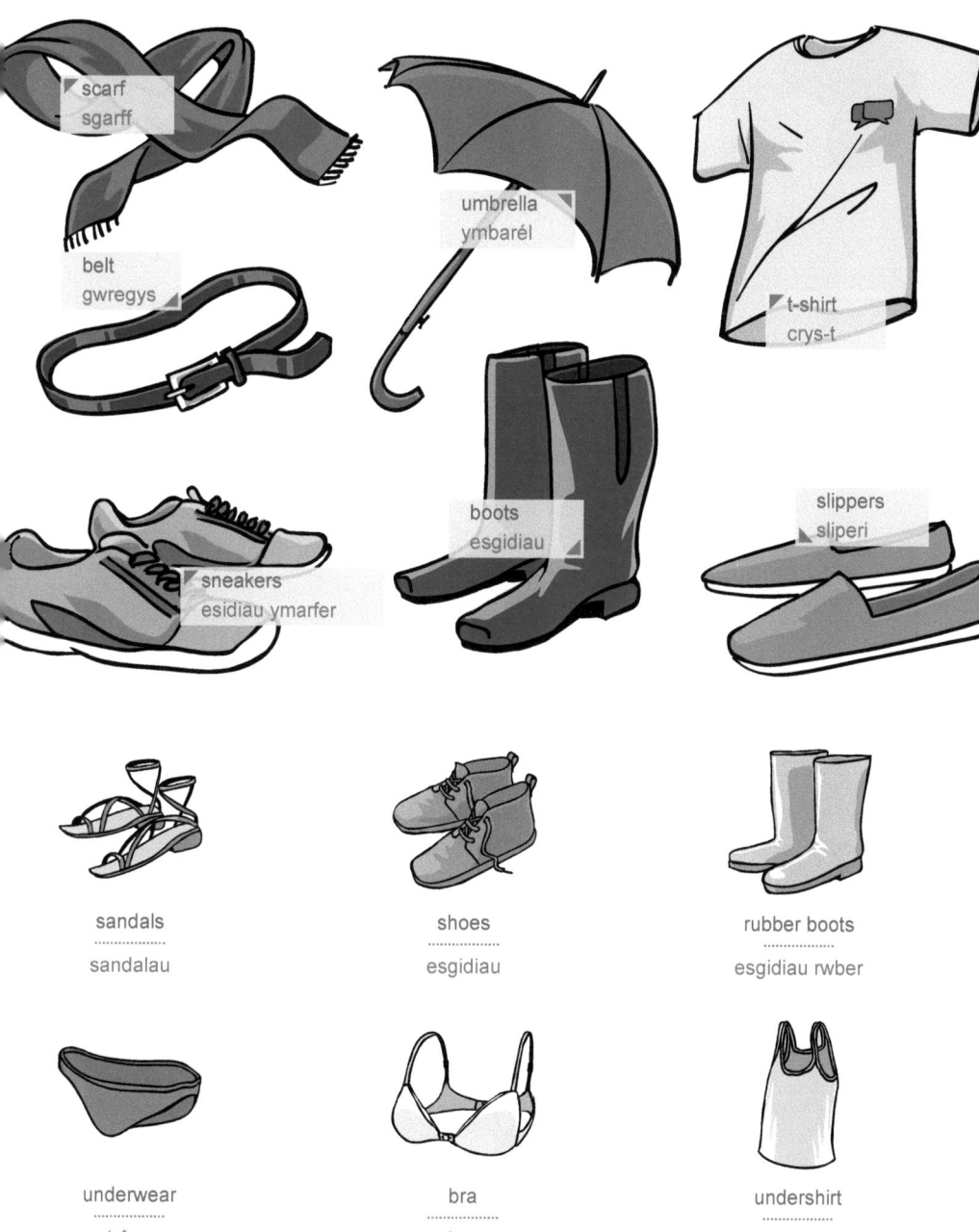

scarf
sgarff

umbrella
ymbarél

t-shirt
crys-t

belt
gwregys

boots
esgidiau

slippers
sliperi

sneakers
esidiau ymarfer

sandals
sandalau

shoes
esgidiau

rubber boots
esgidiau rwber

underwear
trôns

bra
bra

undershirt
fest

clothing - dillad

45

body

corff

pants

trowsus

jeans

jîns

skirt

sgert

blouse

blows

shirt

crys

pullover

pwlofer

sweater

hwdi

blazer

blaser

jacket

siaced

coat

côt

raincoat

côt law

costume

gwisg

dress

gŵn

wedding dress

gwisg briodas

suit

siwt

nightgown

gŵn nos

pajamas

pyjamas

sari

sari

headscarf

sgarff pen

turban

tyrban

burka

bwrca

kaftan

cafftan

abaya

abaya

swimsuit

gwisg nofio

trunks

trowsus nofio

shorts

siorts

tracksuit

tracwisg

apron

ffedog

gloves

menig

button

botwm

glasses

sbectol

bracelet

breichled

necklace

cadwyn

ring

modrwy

earring

clustdlws

cap

cap

coat hanger

cambren

hat

het

tie

tei

zip

sip

helmet

helmed

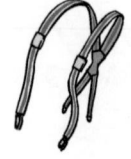

braces

fframiau danedd

school uniform

gwisg ysgol

uniform

gwisg

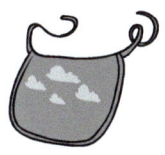

bib

bib

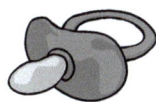

pacifier

teth lwgu

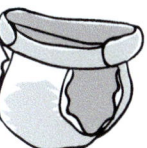

diaper

cewyn

office
swyddfa

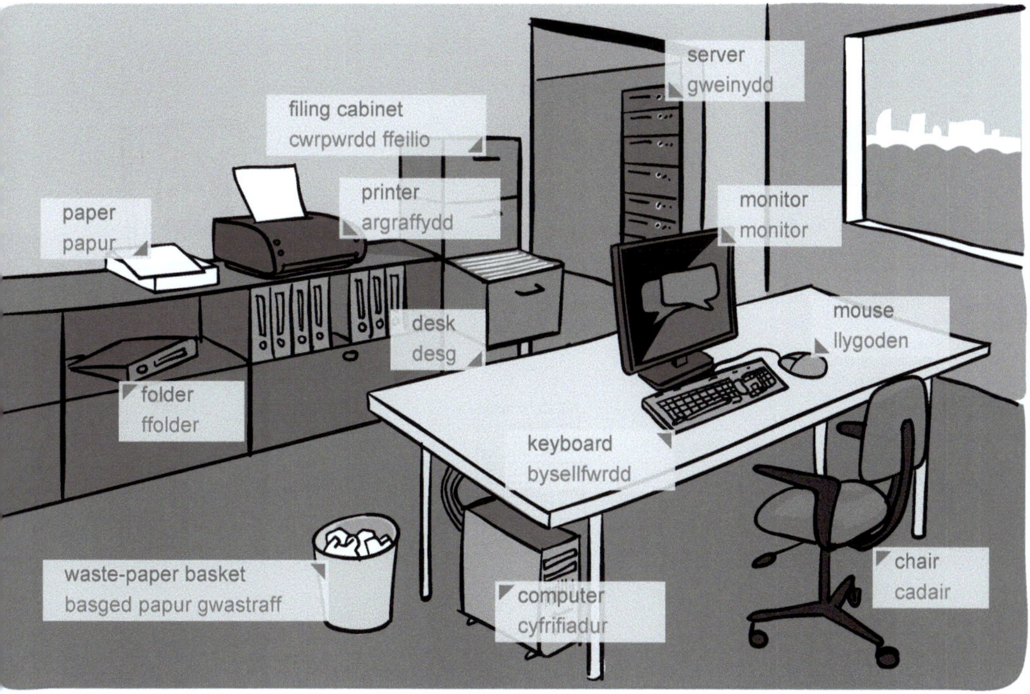
server
gweinydd
filing cabinet
cwrpwrdd ffeilio
paper
papur
printer
argraffydd
monitor
monitor
mouse
llygoden
desk
desg
folder
ffolder
keyboard
bysellfwrdd
waste-paper basket
basged papur gwastraff
computer
cyfrifiadur
chair
cadair

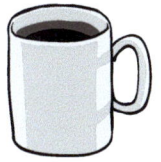

coffee mug

mwg coffi

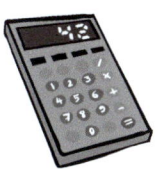

calculator

cyfrifiannell

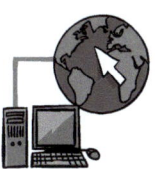

internet

rhyngrwyd

laptop

gliniadur

letter

llythyr

message

neges

cell phone

ffôn symudol

network

rhwydwaith

photocopier

llungopïwr

software

meddalwedd

telephone

teleffon

plug socket

soced plwg

fax machine

peiriant ffacs

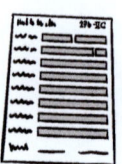

form

ffurflen

document

dogfen

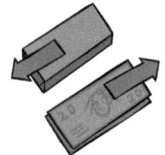

buy

prynu

pay

talu

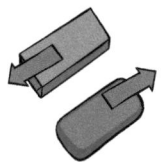

trade

masnachu

money

arian

USD

dollar

doler

EUR

euro

ewro

JPY

yen

yen

RUB

rouble

rwbl

CHF

Swiss franc

ffranc y Swistir

CNY

renminbi yuan

yuan renminbi

INR

rupee

rwpi

cash point

peiriant arian

currency exchange office

swyddfa gyfnewid

gold

aur

silver

arian

oil

olew

energy

ynni

price

pris

contract

contract

tax

treth

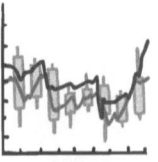

stock

stoc

work

gweithio

employee

cyflogai

employer

cyflogwr

factory

ffatri

shop

siop

police officer
swyddog heddlu

fireman
diffoddwr tân

cook
cogydd

doctor
meddyg

pilot
peilot

gardener
garddwr

carpenter
saer

seamstress
gwniadwraig

judge
barnwr

chemist
fferyllydd

actor
actor

bus driver

gyrrwr bws

taxi driver

gyrrwr tacsi

fisherman

pysgotwr

cleaning lady

glanhawraig

roofer

töwr

waiter

gweinydd

hunter

heliwr

painter

paentiwr

baker

pobydd

electrician

trydanwr

builder

adeiladwr

engineer

peiriannydd

butcher

cigydd

plumber

plymiwr

postman

dyn y post

soldier

milwr

architect

pensaer

cashier

ariannwr

florist

gwerthwr blodau

hairdresser

triniwr gwallt

conductor

archwiliwr tocynnau
rheilffordd

mechanic

mecanydd

captain

capten

dentist

deintydd

scientist

gwyddonydd

rabbi

rabi

imam

imam

monk

mynach

pastor

clerigwr

tools
offer

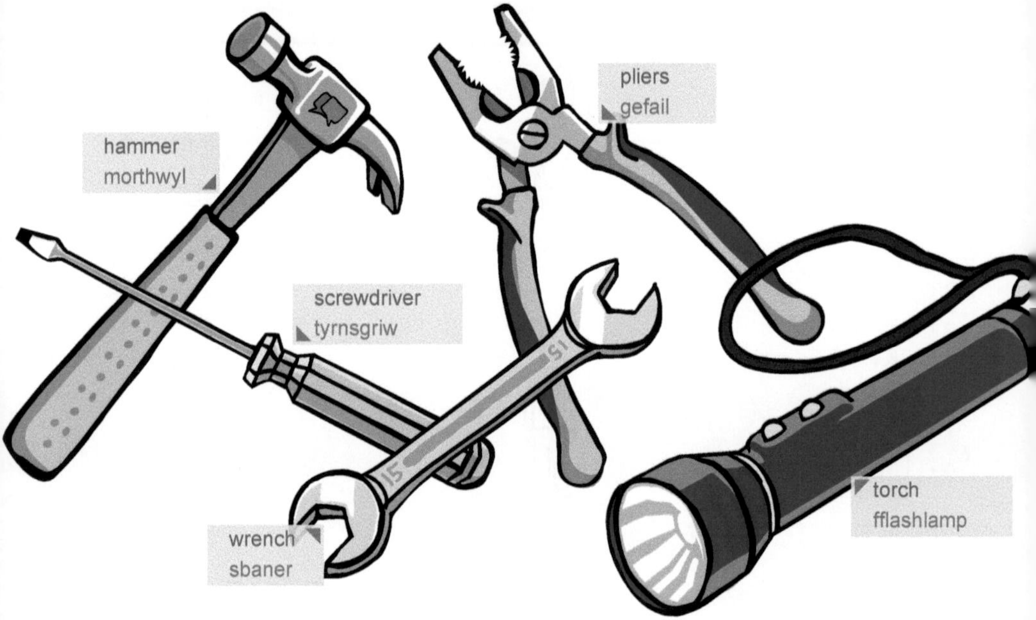
hammer
morthwyl
pliers
gefail
screwdriver
tyrnsgriw
wrench
sbaner
torch
fflashlamp

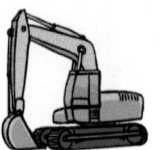

excavator
turiwr

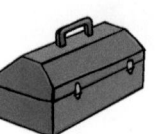

toolbox
blwch offer

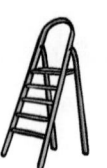

ladder
ysgol

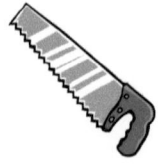

saw
llif

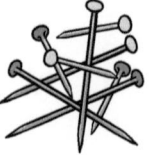

nails
hoelion

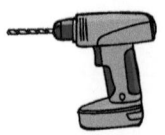

drill
dril

repair

trwsio

shovel

rhaw

Damn!

Daria!

dustpan

rhaw lwch

paint can

pot paent

screws

sgriwiau

musical instruments
offerynnau cerdd

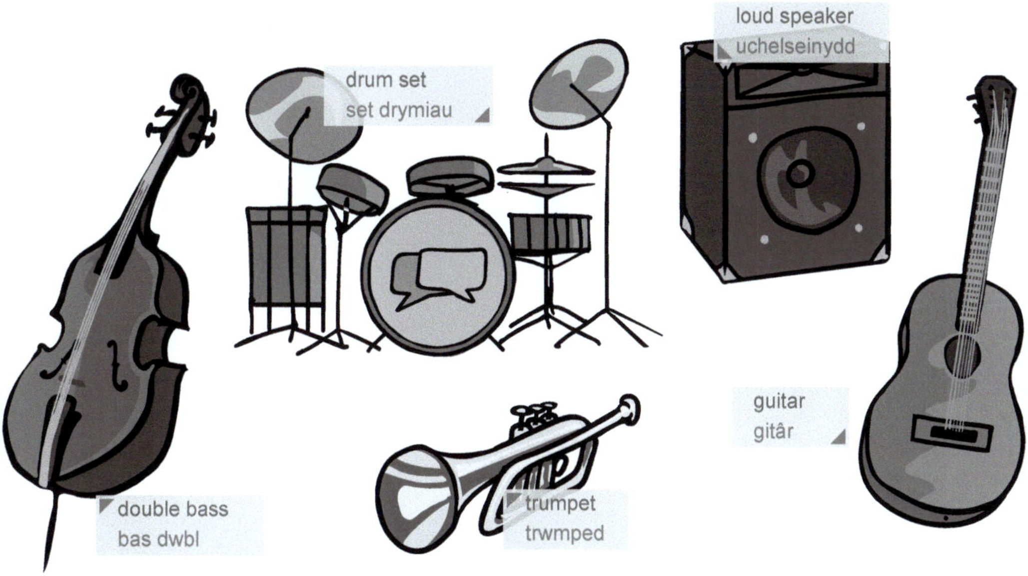

loud speaker
uchelseinydd

drum set
set drymiau

guitar
gitâr

double bass
bas dwbl

trumpet
trwmped

piano

piano

violin

ffidil

bass

bas

timpani

timpani

drums

drymiau

keyboard

cyweirfwrdd

saxophone

sacsoffon

flute

ffliwt

microphone

meicroffon

ZOO

SŴ

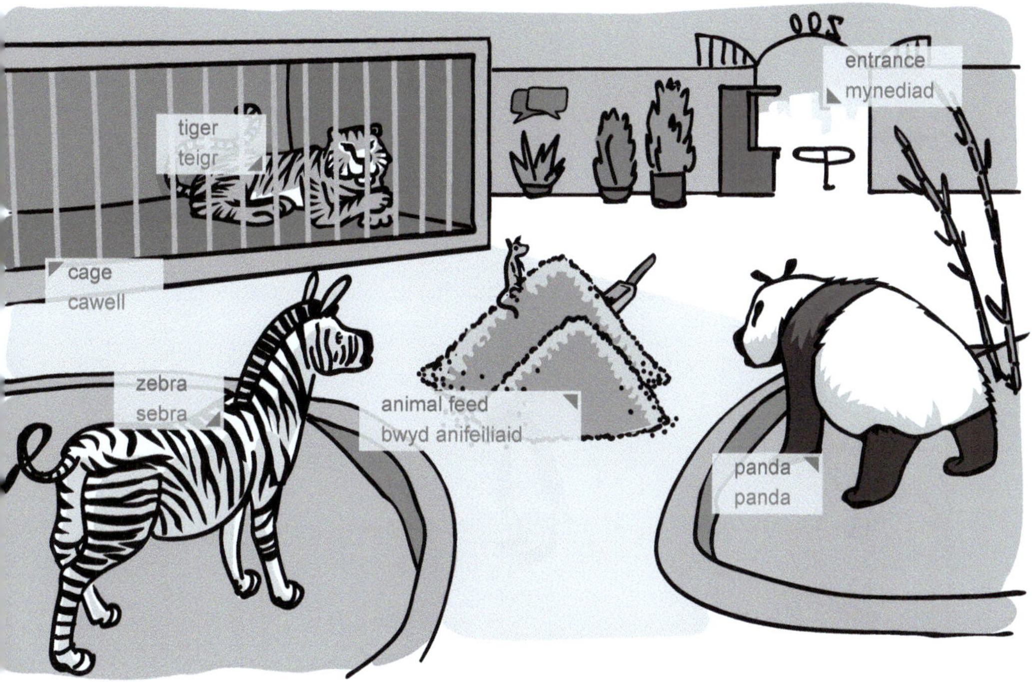

zoo
entrance
mynediad
tiger
teigr
cage
cawell
zebra
sebra
animal feed
bwyd anifeiliaid
panda
panda

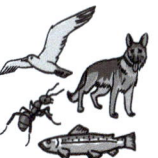

animals
anifeiliaid

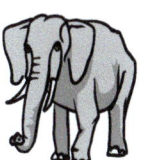

elephant
eliffant

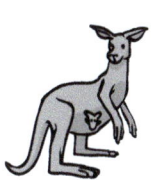

kangaroo
cangarŵ

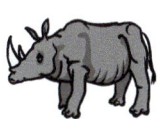

rhino
rhinoseros

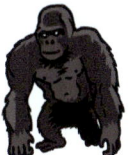

gorilla
gorila

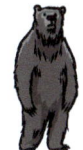

bear
arth

camel

camel

ostrich

estrys

lion

llew

monkey

mwnci

flamingo

fflamingo

parrot

parot

polar bear

arth wen

penguin

pengwin

shark

siarc

peacock

paun

snake

neidr

crocodile

crocodeil

zookeeper

gofalwr sŵ

seal

morlo

jaguar

jagwar

pony

merlyn

leopard

llewpard

hippo

hipo

giraffe

jiráff

eagle

eryr

boar

baedd

fish

pysgodyn

turtle

crwban

walrus

walrws

fox

llwynog

gazelle

gafrewig

American football
pêl-droed America

cycling
beicio

tennis
tennis

basketball
pêl-fasged

swimming
nofio

boxing
bocsio

ice hockey
hoci iâ

soccer

pêl-droed

badminton

badminton

athletics

athletau

handball

pêl-law

skiing

sgïo

polo

polo

jump
neidio

hug
cofleidio

laugh
chwerthin

walk
cerdded

sing
canu

pray
gweddïo

kiss
cusanu

dream
breuddwydio

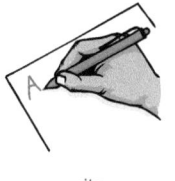

write

ysgrifennu

draw

tynnu

show

dangos

push

gwthio

give

rhoi

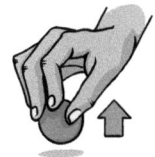

take

cymryd

have

bod gan

do

gwneud

be

bod

stand

sefyll

run

rhedeg

pull

tynnu

throw

taflu

fall

disgyn

lie

gorwedd

wait

aros

carry

cario

sit

eistedd

get dressed

gwisgo amdanoch

sleep

cysgu

wake up

deffro

look at

edrych ar

cry

crïo

stroke

anwesu

comb

cribo

talk

siarad

understand

deall

ask

gofyn

listen

gwrando

drink

yfed

eat

bwyta

tidy up

tacluso

love

caru

cook

coginio

drive

gyrru

fly

hedfan

activities - gweithgareddau

sail

hwylio

calculate

cyfrifo

read

darllen

learn

dysgu

work

gweithio

marry

priodi

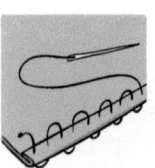

sew

gwnïo

brush teeth

brwsio dannedd

kill

lladd

smoke

ysmygu

send

anfon

family
teulu

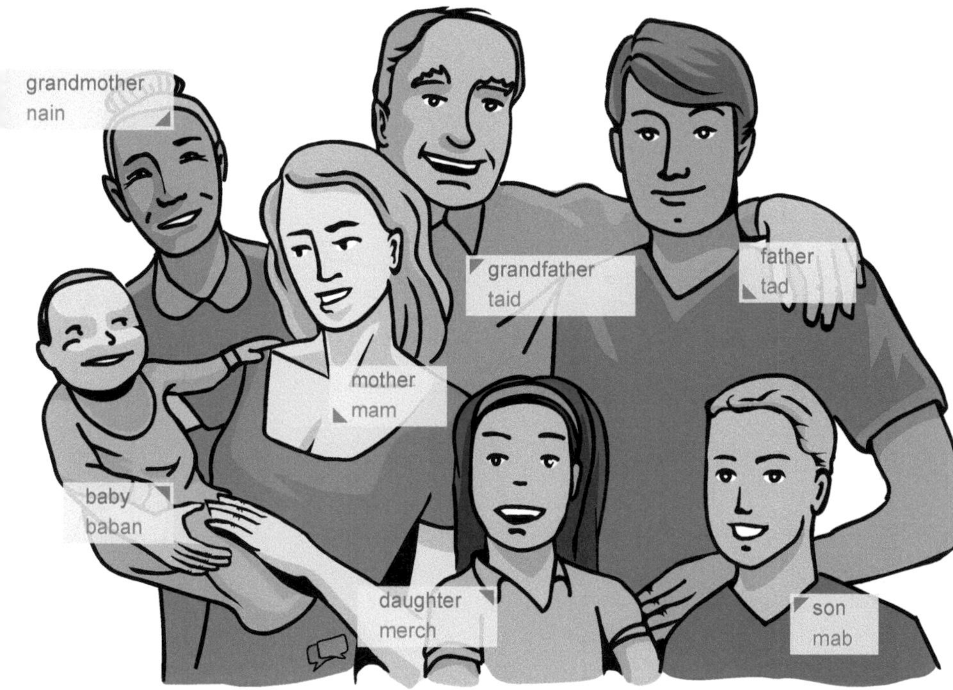
grandmother
nain
grandfather
taid
father
tad
mother
mam
baby
baban
daughter
merch
son
mab

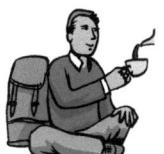

guest

gwestai

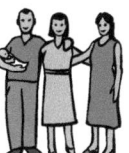

aunt

modryb

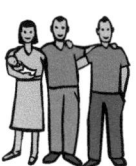

uncle

ewythr

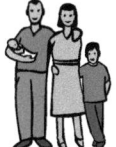

brother

brawd

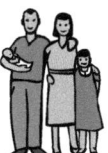

sister

chwaer

body

corff

forehead
talcen
eye
llygad
shoulder
ysgwydd
finger
bys
face
wyneb
chin
gên
hand
llaw
leg
coes
breast
bron
arm
braich

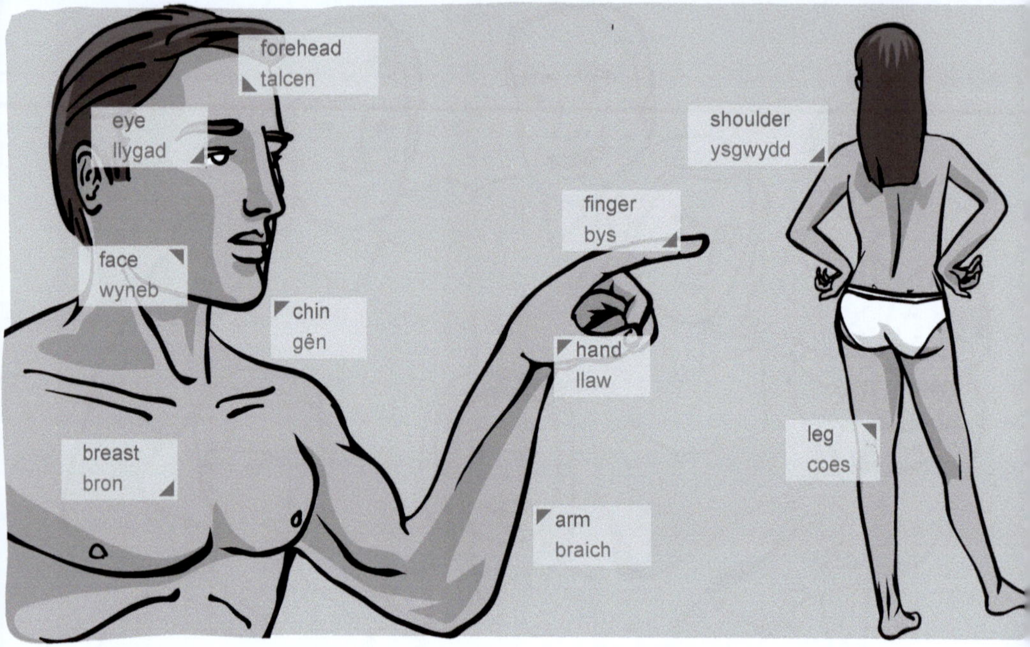

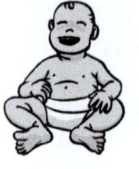

baby

baban

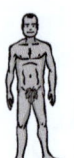

man

dyn

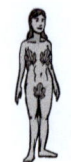

woman

gwraig

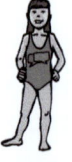

girl

geneth

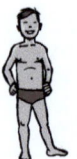

boy

bachgen

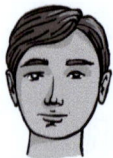

head

pen

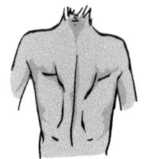

back

cefn

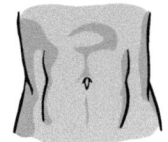

belly

bel

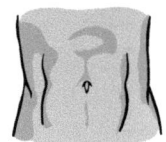

navel

bogail

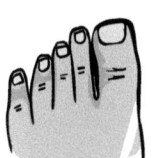

toe

bys troed

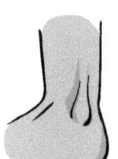

heel

sawdl

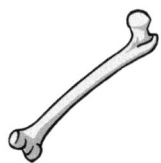

bone

asgwrn

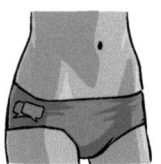

hip

clun

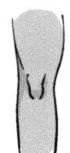

knee

pen-glin

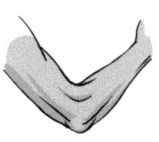

elbow

penelin

nose

trwyn

buttocks

pen ôl

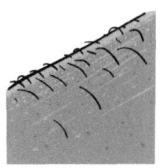

skin

croen

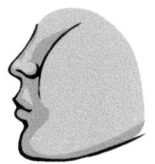

cheek

boch

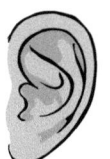

ear

clust

lip

gwefus

mouth

ceg

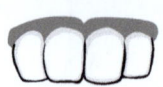

tooth

dant

tongue

tafod

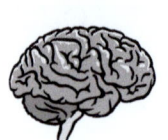

brain

ymennydd

heart

calon

muscle

cyhyr

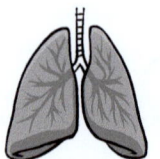

lung

ysgyfaint

liver

iau

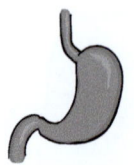

stomach

stumog

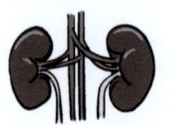

kidneys

arennau

sex

rhyw

condom

condom

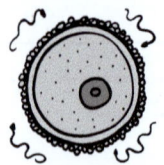

ovum

ofwm

semen

semen

pregnancy

beichiogrwydd

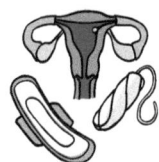

menstruation

mislif

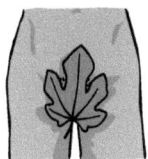

vagina

fagina

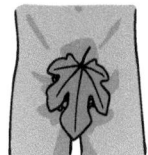

penis

pidyn

eyebrow

ael

hair

gwallt

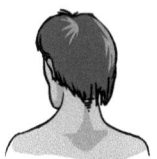

neck

gwddf

hospital

ysbyty

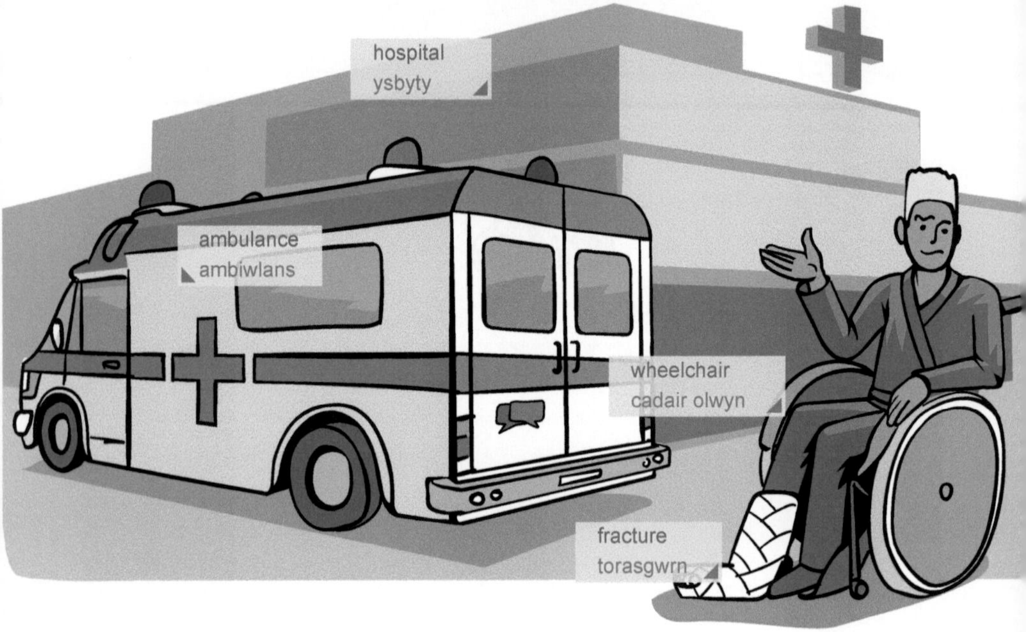

hospital
ysbyty
ambulance
ambiwlans
wheelchair
cadair olwyn
fracture
torasgwrn

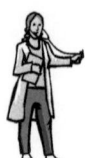

doctor

meddyg

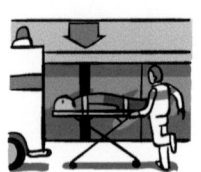

emergency room

ystafell argyfwng

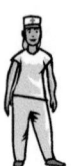

nurse

nyrs

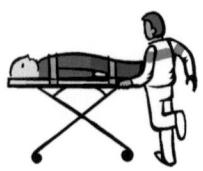

emergency

argyfwng

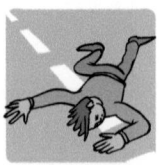

unconscious

anymwybodol

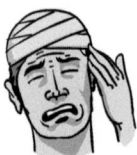

pain

poen

injury

anaf

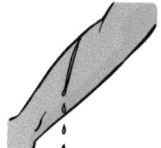

bleeding

gwaedu

heart attack

trawiad ar y galon

stroke

strôc

allergy

alergedd

cough

peswch

fever

twymyn

flu

ffliw

diarrhea

dolur rhydd

headache

cur pen

cancer

canser

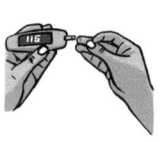

diabetes

diabetes

surgeon

llawfeddyg

scalpel

fflaim

operation

gweithrediad

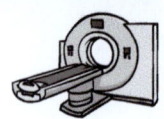

CT

CT

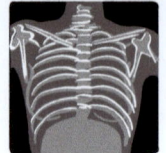

x-ray

pelydr-x

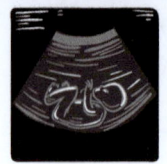

ultrasound

uwchsain

face mask

mwgwd wyneb

disease

clefyd

waiting room

ystafell aros

crutch

bagl

plaster

plastr

bandage

rhwymyn

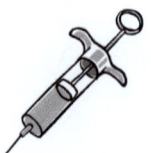

injection

pigiad

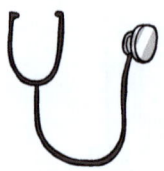

stethoscope

stethosgop

stretcher

elorwely

clinical thermometer

thermomedr clinigol

birth

genedigaeth

overweight

dros bwysau

hearing aid

cymorth clyw

disinfectant

diheintydd

infection

haint

virus

firws

HIV / AIDS

HIV / AIDS

medicine

meddygaeth

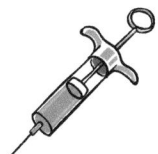

vaccination

brechiad

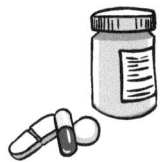

tablets

tabledi

pill

y bilsen

emergency call

galwad frys

blood pressure monitor

monitor pwysau gwaed

ill / healthy

yn sâl / yn iach

Help!
Help!

alarm
larwm

assault
ymosodiad

attack
ymosodiad

danger
perygl

emergency exit
allanfa argyfwng

Fire!
Tân!

fire extinguisher
diffoddwr tân

accident
damwain

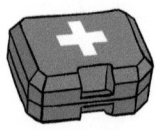

first-aid kit
pecyn cymorth cyntaf

SOS
SOS

police
heddlu

Europe

Ewrop

North America

Gogledd America

South America

De America

Africa

Affrica

Asia

Asia

Australia

Awstralia

Atlantic

Iwerydd

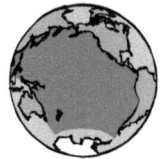

Pacific

y Môr Tawel

Indian Ocean

Cefnfor yr India

Antarctic Ocean

Cefnfor yr Antarctig

Arctic Ocean

Cefnfor yr Arctig

North pole

Pegwn y Gogledd

South pole

Pegwn y De

Antarctica

Antarctica

earth

y Ddaear

land

tir

sea

môr

island

ynys

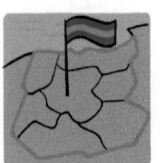

nation

cenedl

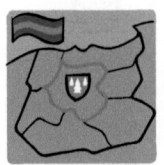

state

gwladwriaeth

clock face

wyneb cloc

hour hand

bys awr

minute hand

bys munud

second hand

bys eiliad

What time is it?

Faint o'r gloch yw hi?

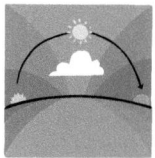

day

dydd

time

amser

now

yn awr

digital watch

cloc digidol

minute

munud

hour

awr

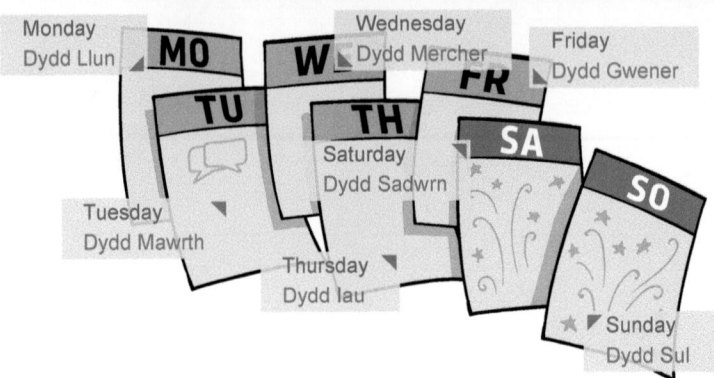

Monday
Dydd Llun

Wednesday
Dydd Mercher

Friday
Dydd Gwener

Tuesday
Dydd Mawrth

Saturday
Dydd Sadwrn

Thursday
Dydd Iau

Sunday
Dydd Sul

yesterday

ddoe

today

heddiw

tomorrow

yfory

morning

bore

noon

canol dydd

evening

noswaith

workdays

diwrnodiau busnes

weekend

penwythnos

year

blwyddyn

rain
glaw
spring
gwanwyn
summer
haf
wind
gwynt
fall
hydref
snow
eira
winter
gaeaf

4.APRIL 11°
5.APRIL 4°
6.APRIL 13°
7.APRIL 8°
8.APRIL 10°

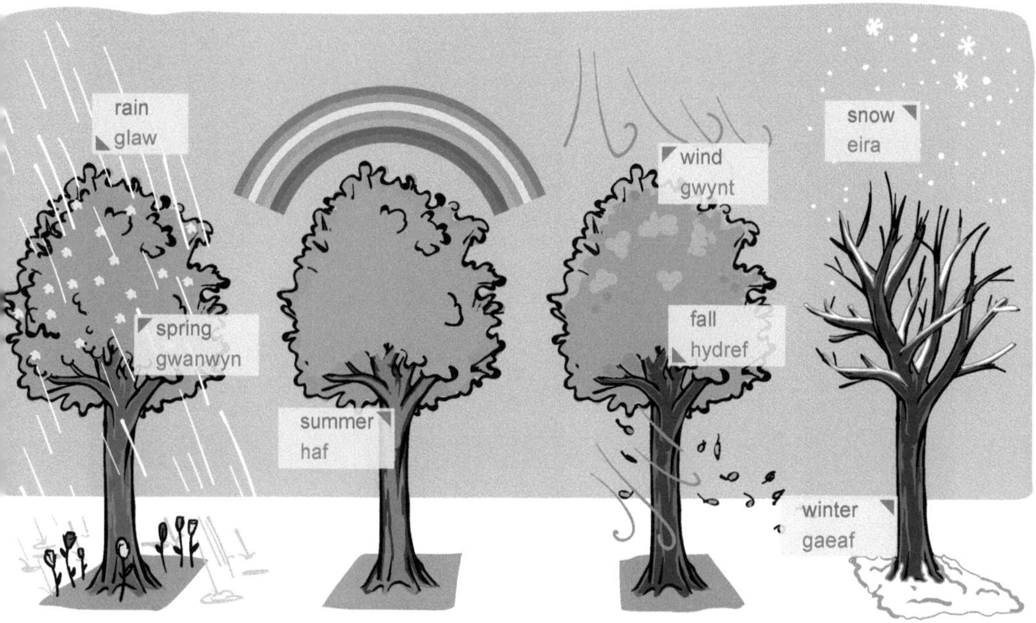

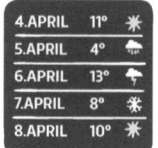

weather forecast

rhagolygon y tywydd

F C
120 90 60 30 0 -30
40 30 20 10 0 -10 -20

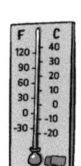

thermometer

thermomedr

sunshine

heulwen

cloud

cwmwl

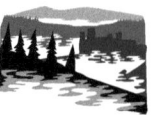

fog

niwl tew

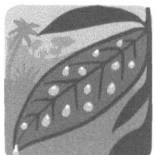

humidity

lleithder

lightning

mellt

thunder

taranau

storm

storm

hail

cenllysg

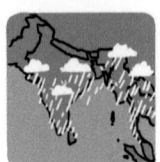

monsoon

monswˆn

flood

llif

ice

iâ

January

Ionawr

February

Chwefror

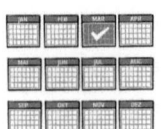

March

Mawrth

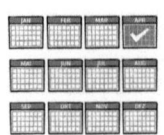

April

Ebrill

May

Mai

June

Mehefin

July

Gorffennaf

August

Awst

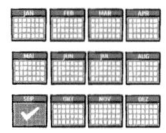

September

Medi

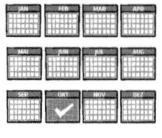

October

Hydref

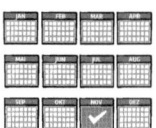

November

Tachwedd

December

Rhagfyr

shapes
siapiau

circle

cylch

square

sgwâr

rectangle

petryal

triangle

triongl

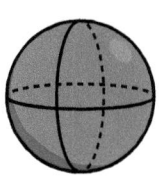

sphere

sffêr

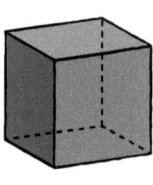

cube

ciwb

white
....
gwyn

yellow
....
melyn

orange
....
oren

pink
....
pinc

red
....
coch

purple
....
porffor

blue
....
glas

green
....
gwyrdd

brown
....
brown

gray
....
llwyd

black
....
du

a lot / a little

llawer / ychydig

angry / calm

dig / tawel

beautiful / ugly

hardd / hyll

beginning / end

dechrau / diwedd

big / small

mawr / bach

bright / dark

llachar / tywyll

brother / sister

brawd / chwaer

clean / dirty

glân / budr

complete / incomplete

gyflawn / anghyflawn

day / night

dydd / nos

dead / alive

farw / yn fyw

wide / narrow

eang / cul

edible / inedible

bwytadwy / anfwytadwy

evil / kind

drwg / caredig

excited / bored

llawn cyffro / diflasu

fat / thin

tew / tenau

first / last

cyntaf / olaf

friend / enemy

cyfaill / gelyn

full / empty

llawn / gwag

hard / soft

caled / meddal

heavy / light

trwm / ysgafn

hunger / thirst

wedi newynnu / yn sychedig

ill / healthy

yn sâl / yn iach

illegal / legal

anghyfreithlon / cyfreithiol

intelligent / stupid

deallus / twp

left / right

chwith / dde

near / far

agos / pell

new / used

newydd / wedi'i ddefnyddio

nothing / something

dim / rhywbeth

old / young

hen / ifanc

on / off

ymlaen / i ffwrdd

open / closed

ar agor / ar gau

quiet / loud

tawel / uchel

rich / poor

cyfoethog / tlawd

right / wrong

cywir / anghywir

rough / smooth

garw / llyfn

sad / happy

trist / hapus

short / long

byr / hir

slow / fast

araf / cyflym

wet / dry

gwlyb / sych

warm / cool

cynnes / claear

war / peace

rhyfel / heddwch

0

zero

sero

1

one

un

2

two

dau

3

three

tri

4

four

pedwar

5

five

pump

6

six

chwech

7

seven

saith

8

eight

wyth

9

nine

naw

10

ten

deg

11

eleven

un deg un

12

twelve

un deg dau

13

thirteen

un deg tri

14

fourteen

un deg pedwar

15

fifteen

un deg pump

16

sixteen

un deg chwech

17

seventeen

un deg saith

18

eighteen

un deg wyth

19

nineteen

un deg naw

20

twenty

dau ddeg

100

hundred

cant

1.000

thousand

mil

1.000.000

million

miliwn

English

Saesneg

American English

Saesneg America

Chinese Mandarin

Tsieinëeg Mandarin

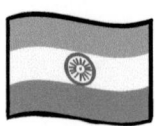

Hindi

Hindi

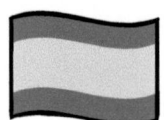

Spanish

Sbaeneg

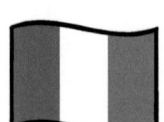

French

Ffrangeg

Arabic

Arabeg

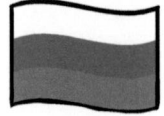

Russian

Rwseg

Portuguese

Portiwgaleg

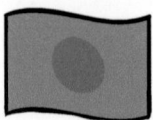

Bengali

Bengali

German

Almaeneg

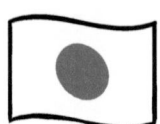

Japanese

Siapanaeg

I

fi

you

ti

he / she / it

ef / hi

we

ni

you

chi

they

nhw

who?

pwy?

what?

beth?

how?

sut?

where?

ble?

when?

pryd?

name

enw

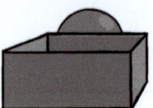

behind

y tu ôl i

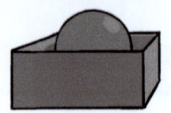

in

yn / yng / ym / mewn

in front of

o flaen

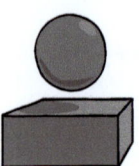

over

dros

on

ar

under

dan

beside

wrth ochr

between

rhwng

place

lle